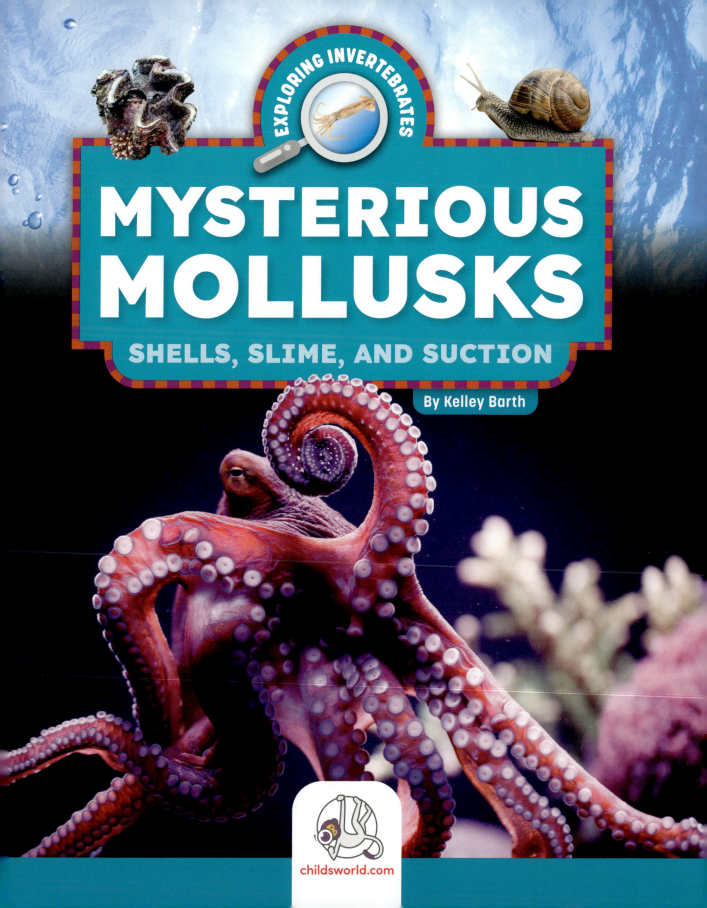

Published by The Child's World®
800-599-READ • childsworld.com

Copyright © 2025 by The Child's World®
All rights reserved. No part of this book may be reproduced or utilized in any form or by any means without written permission from the publisher.

Photography Credits
Cover: ©alonanola/Shutterstock; ©Jiang Zhongyan /Shutterstock; ©Georgy Dzyura/Shutterstock; ©Shin Okamoto Shutterstock; ©Reynold Mainse/Design Pics/Getty Images ©Eric Isselee/Shutterstock; ©zcw/Shutterstock; pages 3, 12–13, 14: ©Romulo Tavani/Shutterstock; pages 3, 4, 21, 24: ©Gregory Dzyura/Shutterstock; pages 3, 15: ©zcw/Shutterstock; page 5: ©nete.rpp/Shutterstock; page 5: ©Placebo 365/Getty Images; page 5: ©Sebastian Kaulitzki/Science Photo Library/Getty Images; page 6: ©Alice Cahill/Getty Images; page 6: ©Busybee-CR/Getty Images; page 7: ©Eric Isselee/Shutterstock; page 9: ©Marc Andreu/Shutterstock; page 9: ©Mike Kemp/Getty Images; page 11: ©Subaqueossshutterbug/Getty Images; page 13: ©Tamil Selvam/Shutterstock; page 14: ©alonanola/Shutterstock; page 14: ©Emmy Ilham/Shutterstock; page 14: ©Shiraufa's Art/Shutterstock; page 14: ©Gerard Soury/Getty Images: page 16: ©Henner Damke/Shutterstock; page 17: ©Andreas Furil/Getty Images; page 18–19: ©topimages/Shutterstock; page 20: ©Aleksei Permiakov/Getty Images

ISBN Information
9781503894501 (Reinforced Library Binding)
9781503894778 (Portable Document Format)
9781503895591 (Online Multi-user eBook)
9781503896413 (Electronic Publication)

LCCN
2024941437

Printed in the United States of America

ABOUT THE AUTHOR

Kelley Barth is a former children's librarian who loves connecting with young people over stories and books. When she isn't busy writing, she enjoys reading, hiking, crafting, and going on adventures with her husband and son.

CHAPTER 1
MEET THE MOLLUSK . . . 4

CHAPTER 2
MOLLUSK BODIES . . . 8

CHAPTER 3
THE LIFE CYCLE OF A MOLLUSK . . . 12

CHAPTER 4
MOLLUSKS IN THE WORLD . . . 18

CHAPTER 5
THE FUTURE OF MOLLUSKS . . . 20

Wonder More . . . 21
Safe Shells . . . 22
Glossary . . . 23
Find Out More . . . 24
Index . . . 24

CHAPTER 1

MEET THE MOLLUSK

An oyster rests on a rock along the ocean shore. Inside its shell, a grain of sand slowly turns into a pearl. A snail snacks on leaves in a garden. It leaves a trail of slime as it moves. A squid floats deep in the ocean. It reaches out a **tentacle** to grab its **prey**. These animals look different from each other. They move in different ways. They eat different foods. They live in your backyard and at the bottom of the ocean. But they all have one important thing in common. They are all mollusks!

MOLLUSK SIZE COMPARISON

Squids come in all shapes and sizes! The colossal squid can be almost 60 feet (18.3 meters) long. Its eye is the size of a standard soccer ball!

The pygmy squid can be as small as 0.04 inches (1 millimeter) long, but some grow as big as 0.8 inches (2 centimeters). They are often mistaken for baby squids.

colossal squid　　　　　　　　　**pygmy squid**

A giant clam can weigh up to 500 pounds (227 kilograms). These huge creatures are found in the South Pacific and Indian Oceans.

The large hole on the right side of a banana slug's head allows it to breathe. It opens and closes, much like a whale's blowhole.

Gray garden slugs are found in many lawns and gardens. They are easy to spot by the trail of slime they leave behind.

Mollusks are found on every continent except Antarctica. They live in almost every type of habitat. Most live in the ocean. Some live in fresh water such as rivers, streams, or lakes. A few mollusks, including snails and slugs, live on land. They live in rainforests, mountains, and even deserts. Mollusks are everywhere! No matter where they live, mollusks must stay **moist**. Mollusks that live on land are covered in slime. This slime keeps them from drying out. Slime also helps them move. Most mollusks are **nocturnal**. They sleep during the day and are awake at night.

CHAPTER 2
MOLLUSK BODIES

Mollusks are different shapes, sizes, and colors. They have soft bodies with no bones. All mollusks have a **mantle**. The mantle is skin that protects their body. Many mollusks have hard shells. Shells cover the mantle. Most mollusks have a **radula**. A radula is like a tongue. It is rough with many tiny teeth. It helps mollusks eat. Mollusks also have a strong muscle that helps them move. It is called a foot. Sea slugs crawl on the ocean floor with their foot. Clams use their foot to dig into dirt or sand. Some animals have many arms instead of one foot.

PARTS OF A SNAIL

- eyes
- head
- tentacles
- shell
- mouth
- foot
- mantle

MOLLUSKS ON THE MOVE

Slime isn't the only way mollusks move. Squids suck in water and push it back out. This helps them swim fast. Scallops move in a similar way. Clapping their shells together pushes out water. This moves them forward. Octopuses can swim through the water or crawl on the ocean floor. Clams burrow into mud or sand. Other mollusks don't move at all. Oysters attach themselves to rocks or other shells and stay there.

The blue-ringed octopus is fun to look at, but its venom is deadly. Fortunately, they usually only use their venom to capture and kill their food.

Many animals eat mollusks. But mollusks can protect themselves. Hard shells keep many mollusks safe. Snails can hide inside their shell if a hungry bird is near.

Not all mollusks have shells, though. They need other tricks to stay safe. Many sea slugs are brightly colored. Their colors warn other animals to stay away. Animals such as cuttlefish use **camouflage**. They change their color and texture to hide. Most squids and octopuses can shoot ink. This helps them escape danger. The blue-ringed octopus goes one step further. It is **venomous**. One bite can kill a **predator**.

CHAPTER 3

THE LIFE CYCLE OF A MOLLUSK

There are three main types of mollusks. **Gastropods** are the most common. Gastropod means "stomach foot." Their stomachs are right above their foot muscles. Snails and slugs are gastropods. Snails have shells. Slugs do not. All gastropods have a head. They usually have tentacles with eyes. Most snails and slugs eat plants. A few eat other animals. Snails and slugs lay eggs. The eggs hatch and grow into adults. Most gastropods only live for about one year. But some can live more than 20 years.

The nudibranch (NOO-deh-brank) is commonly known as a sea slug. They come in a variety of shapes and colors, and they are very delicate.

LIFE CYCLE OF A GIANT CLAM

A giant clam can live up to 100 years. It goes through many stages of life.

Spawn Stage:
An adult releases eggs and sperm.

Larvae Stage:
Larvae float and seek out food.

Adult Clam

Juvenile Stage:
The animal changes shape, growing a shell and foot. The clam settles in one spot.

Some mollusks are **bivalves**. Bivalves have two shells. The shells connect with a hinge. Clams, oysters, scallops, and mussels are bivalves. Strong muscles help them open and close their shells. Bivalves do not have heads. But they can still eat. They have two tubes on their backside. One tube pulls in small bits of food. The second tube pumps out waste. These tubes filter the water they live in. Bivalves start out as eggs. Eggs grow into **larvae**. Larvae float free in the water. When they are big enough, they change into adults.

The smartest and fastest type of mollusks are **cephalopods** (SEF-uh-loh-podz). Octopuses and squids are cephalopods. Most cephalopods do not have shells. These animals have large heads and good eyesight. They also have a beak, just like a parrot. This helps them eat. Cephalopods have many strong foot muscles. Their feet are called arms because they are attached to their head. Most have 8 or 10 arms. But the nautilus can have up to 90! Cephalopods eat meat and hunt for food. Suckers on their arms help them grab and hold on to prey. A female octopus will protect her eggs for months or even years before they hatch. But most cephalopods die soon after their young are born.

SMARTS IN THE SEA

Cephalopods are very smart. Octopuses in zoos and aquariums have opened jars and untied knots. They can solve simple problems and use tools. But there is another trick that octopuses are famous for. They can escape almost anything. Even a big octopus can fit through very tiny spaces. One octopus escaped from his aquarium back into the ocean. It helps to not have any bones!

The giant Pacific octopus has around 280 suckers on each of its eight arms. That's more than 2,200 suction cups on a single octopus!

CHAPTER 4

MOLLUSKS IN THE WORLD

Mollusks are important animals in our world. They are a part of the food chain. Many animals and people eat mollusks. Humans also use mollusks for other reasons. Mollusk shells are very beautiful. People collect them to make jewelry.

Mollusks help the environment. Snails and slugs break down dead plants and animals. This helps soil stay healthy. Animals such as oysters filter ocean water. This can lessen pollution. But some mollusks can cause problems, too. Red slugs eat food crops. Zebra mussels clog up water pipes and cause damage for humans. These animals are known as **invasive species**.

Oyster farms don't just supply the seafood industry. They filter millions of gallons of water a day.

CHAPTER 5

THE FUTURE OF MOLLUSKS

Mollusks have existed for millions of years. Today, they live all around us. More than 100,000 different kinds of mollusks have been found in nature. Scientists are discovering new mollusks all the time! Mollusks also help inspire science. Scientists are studying how squid ink can be used as medicine. Others are creating medical tools that work like octopus suckers. Whether they are tucked into a riverbed or hidden on the ocean floor, we still have a lot to learn from mollusks.

WONDER MORE

Wondering About New Information

What new information did you learn about mollusks? Write down three new facts you learned. Did this information surprise you? Why or why not?

Wondering How It Matters

Mollusks play important roles in our world. What are some of the ways mollusks impact your life? How would the world be different if we didn't have mollusks?

Wondering Why

Mollusks have many ways of protecting themselves. What are some of the ways mollusks stay safe? What are some ways that other animals and people stay safe? Are there any similarities between people and mollusks?

Ways to Keep Wondering

After reading this book, what questions do you have about mollusks? What can you do to learn more about them?

SAFE SHELLS

Mollusks must stay safe from predators. Some use camouflage to hide or bright colors to scare others away. Most mollusks have shells to help them. Create your own shell that could help keep a mollusk safe.

Steps to Take

1) Decide what type of shell you are going to create. Will it be one spiral shell or two hinged shells?

2) Have an adult help you cut your shell shape out of cardstock.

3) Decorate your shell using craft supplies and other objects. Think about how mollusks use color and texture. Do you want your mollusk to blend into the environment or to stand out?

4) Share your creation and talk about how it will help protect a mollusk!

Supplies
- cardstock
- paper
- scissors
- markers
- a variety of craft supplies (Try yarn, beads, ribbons, aluminum foil, or other objects you find around your home.)

GLOSSARY

bivalves (BY-valvz) Bivalves are a type of mollusk that have two shells joined at a hinge, like clams and oysters.

camouflage (KA-muh-flaazh) Camouflage helps animals disguise themselves to blend into their environment.

cephalopods (SEF-uh-loh-podz) Cephalopods are a type of mollusk with a large head and many arms, like octopuses and squid.

gastropods (GA-struh-paadz) Gastropods are a type of mollusk with a head and tentacles, like snails and slugs.

invasive species (in-VAY-siv SPEE-sheez) Invasive species are animals that have moved to live outside of their native area.

larvae (LAAR-vee) Larvae are the early form of an animal before they change into an adult.

mantle (MAN-tuhl) A mantle is a skin-like covering that protects a mollusk.

moist (MOYST): Moist means to be slightly wet or damp.

nocturnal (nok-TUR-nuhl) Nocturnal animals are awake at night and sleep during the day.

predator (PRED-uh-tur) A predator is an animal that lives by hunting other animals for food.

prey (PRAY) Prey are animals that are hunted and eaten by other animals.

radula (RADJ-uh-luh) A radula is covered in rough, tiny teeth that help mollusks scrape or tear food.

tentacle (TEN-tuh-kul) A tentacle is a thin structure around the head of an animal or insect used for feeling or grasping.

venomous (VEH-nuh-muhs) Venomous animals have poisonous bites.

FIND OUT MORE

In the Library

Clarke, Ginjer L. *Octopus!: Smartest in the Sea?* New York, NY: Penguin Young Readers, 2024.

Owens, L. L. *The Life Cycle of a Snail.* Parker, CO: The Child's World, 2023.

Tyler, Madeline. *Mollusks.* New York, NY: KidHaven Publishing, 2020.

On the Web

Visit our website for links about mollusks:

childsworld.com/links

Note to Parents, Caregivers, Teachers, and Librarians: We routinely verify our web links to make sure they are safe and active sites. So encourage your readers to check them out!

INDEX

arms, 8, 16–17

clam, 5, 8, 10, 14–15

food, 10, 14–16, 18
foot, 4, 10, 14–16, 18

larvae, 14–15

mantle, 8–9

octopus, 10–11, 16–17, 20

shell, 4, 8–12, 18
slime, 4, 6–7, 10
slug, 6–8, 11–13, 18
snail, 4, 7, 9, 11–12, 18
squid, 4–5, 10–11, 16, 20